SUPER CITIES!

HOUSTON

by Michael Burgan

arcadia®
CHILDREN'S BOOKS

Published by Arcadia Children's Books
A Division of Arcadia Publishing
Charleston, SC
www.arcadiapublishing.com

Super Cities is a trademark of Arcadia Publishing, Inc.

First published 2021

ISBN 978-1-5402-5064-3

Library of Congress Control Number: 2021943262

Produced by Shoreline Publishing Group LLC
Santa Barbara, California
Designer: Patty Kelley

Contents

WELCOME TO

Houston!

Texas is one huge state—only Alaska is bigger. And the biggest city in Texas is Houston. With more than 2.3 million people calling Houston home, it's the fourth-largest city in the United States. It's fast on its way to being number three!

What draws so many people to Houston? Work is one answer. Houston is home to major companies that produce oil, gas, and chemicals for the world. The city is also a center for medical research and treatment. And it earned the nickname "Space City" for its role in helping to send astronauts into space—and to the moon! Folks in Houston also enjoy its many museums and art

Houston,
Texas

FAST FACTS
Houston, Texas

POPULATION:
2.3 MILLION

FOUNDED:
1836

NICKNAMES:
**Space City, H-Town,
Bayou City, Clutch City**

centers. And for people who like to relax on a beach, the warm shores of the Gulf of Mexico are just a short drive away.

Houstonians are a diverse bunch. That means they come from many different countries and have a variety of racial, religious, and ethnic backgrounds. All that variety makes Houston a foodie paradise. From thick steaks to Mexican favorites to Asian specialties, you'll never go hungry in Houston!

Let's go, y'all!

Houston (5)

HOUSTON: Map It!

Houston is a sprawling, flat city that covers a lot of ground. It's more than half as big as the entire state of Rhode Island! And this entire list of other big American cities ALL would fit inside Houston's city limits: New York City, Washington DC, Boston, San Francisco, Seattle, Minneapolis, and Miami!

Houston was founded on Buffalo Bayou. A bayou is a small, slow-moving body of water that leads into a larger one. Houston's big bayou flows to the Houston Ship Channel, which leads to Galveston Bay. That bay borders the Gulf of Mexico. Docks along the channel make Houston a major port city. To the east of Houston is a forested area called Piney Woods. Houstonians and tourists alike flock there for hiking, camping, and other outdoor activities.

Houston, Texas

NEW MEXICO

OKLAHOMA

TEXAS

MEXICO

Gulf of Mexico

Houston, Texas

N

Hermann Park

Downtown

Buffalo Bayou

Johnson Space Center

Houston Ship Channel

Galveston Bay

Gulf of Mexico

KEY

City limits

Parks

Set the Scene

The National Aeronautics and Space Administration (NASA) has a home in Houston. At its Johnson Space Center, astronauts train for space missions. At Mission Control, NASA engineers keep an eye on the sky. They track what happens at the International Space Station.

Buffalo Bayou flows through the northern part of Houston. A park named for the bayou follows it for several miles. Houstonians hike and cycle on paths or take their kayaks and canoes out for a spin.

Downtown Houston used to empty out when the workday was done. Now, it's a center of activity day and night. The area is home to Houston's major sports teams, theaters, and an aquarium.

At the Galleria, Houston's major mall, you can do much more than shop till you drop. The gigantic center has hotels, office buildings, two swimming pools, 400 shops, and 60 restaurants.

Looking for a big spot of green in the middle of the city? Head to Hermann Park. Its 445 acres include trails, a golf course, and its own railroad. The park is also filled with art, including a statue of George Hermann. He donated the original park land more than 100 years ago, and the park was named for him.

HOUSTON
MEANS...

If Houston were named for the men who founded it, we'd be calling the city Allenville (more on the Allens on page 17). Instead, the city was named in honor of Sam Houston, one of the most important figures in Texas history.

Sam was a general, a governor, a member of Congress, and a president. Not a US president—he was president of Texas when it was briefly an independent nation. And he made history as the only American to serve as the governor of two states. Before heading west to Texas in 1832, he was the governor of Tennessee.

Today, you can find tributes to Sam all over "his" city. There are schools named for him, and a national forest with his name sits about 50 miles north of Houston.

Texas

Texas governor
Sam Houston

A statue of Sam Houston in the city's Memorial Park.

A TASTE OF THE WILD WEST!

Texas is cattle country, and Houston honors that cowboy heritage with its annual Livestock Show and Rodeo. The event began in 1932. Since then, it's grown to include a parade, live entertainment, and a carnival. The Livestock Show and Rodeo is the largest event of its kind in the world. It takes place over 20 days and two million people show up each year. The event helps raise money to send young Texans to college. Here's some of what you can see at this rip-roaring show.

The rodeo features some of the best riders and ropers from across the United States and Canada. They aren't there just for fun—they can earn up to $50,000 for winning an event!

You don't have to like animals to enjoy the rodeo and livestock show. There's plenty to do at the carnival. Ride a Ferris wheel with air-conditioned cars, munch down corn dogs and cotton candy, or find just about anything deep-fried (including, yes . . . candy bars).

The livestock show features thousands of different farm animals raised by kids and teens. The animals compete to see who is the best example of their breed. A separate show for horses lets them show their running and jumping skills.

Horses lead a big parade when the Livestock show opens each year.

Cowboys and cowgirls can't work on an empty stomach. Long ago, they ate food that came from chuck wagons. Chuck was slang for "food." At the rodeo, teams of horses pull chuck wagons as part of a race. The wagons take sharp turns on just two wheels and can reach speeds of 30 miles per hour.

HISTORY: Early Days

People have been living in southeast Texas for more than 10,000 years. The first Native Americans left behind arrowheads and cutting and scraping tools. In about 1000, the Caddo people settled along the region's rivers. They raised corn, beans, and other crops and hunted in the woods. The women made beautiful pottery. Some of it can be seen today in museums.

The Caddo traded with other tribes as far away as Illinois and Florida. When French explorers came to the region, the Caddo traded with them, too. Over time, the Caddo moved farther west into Texas, as Americans settled near their lands. In 1859, the US government forced the Caddo to move to Oklahoma. Some still live there today.

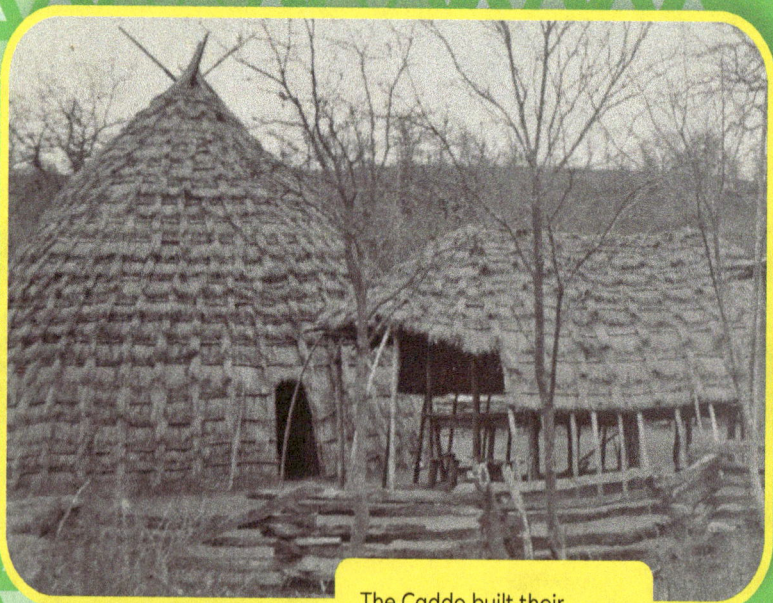

The Caddo built their homes out of layers of dried grass, called thatch. Some of the homes sat on poles.

Pottery used every day was plain. But pottery used for special occasions featured designs.

When their leaders died, the Caddo buried them in large mounds of earth. The Caddo put items in the graves with the dead, such as a sword made of rock.

These moccasins (in a museum in Canada) show the type of beaded designs made by the Caddo people in the 1800s.

HISTORY: Birth of a City

In the early 1800s, Texas was part of Mexico. American settlers began to move into the area. Some of the settlers started a town called Harrisburg in what is now Houston. The town, though, didn't last.

Many Americans and Mexicans in Texas wanted their own country. In 1836, they declared their independence from Mexico—just as Americans had done with Great Britain in 1776. A Mexican army sent to fight the Texans destroyed Harrisburg.

FAST FACT

Texans declared their independence on March 2, 1836. The date is now a state holiday.

April 21, 1836: The Texans fought on. Sam Houston led soldiers that won a major victory over Mexican troops at San Jacinto. The site was about 20 miles away from today's Houston. That win gave the Texans their independence!

People dress as early Texans to put on shows.

John Allen

Augustus Allen

August 1836: Brothers John and Augustus Allen bought land around Buffalo Bayou. They named the town they began building after the war hero Sam Houston. The Allens placed ads in newspapers to attract settlers. They promised that their new town would become a center for trade. Houston was just a small village at the time. Mud often filled the streets, some people lived in tents, and some buildings didn't even have roofs!

Early settlers found fields of bluebonnets, still enjoyed by Houstonians.

1837: Texas leaders made Houston the capital of their new nation. In 1839, though, the capital was moved to Austin.

Along with plenty of mud, early Houstonians had to deal with mosquitos—lots of them! And the buzzing bugs carried a disease called yellow fever. For several decades, the town dealt with waves of the disease. Hundreds of people died each time yellow fever spread. Then, for some unknown reason, after 1870 the disease faded away.

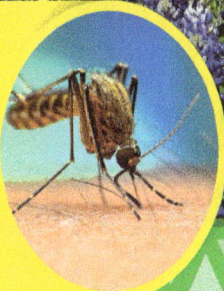

1846: Texas joins the United States as the 28th state. Houston's population was about 2,000.

1853: Despite the fear of yellow fever, Houston slowly grew. Its first railway was built, and farmers shipped cotton and cattle hides out of the city's port. Farmers also grew wheat, rice, and hay, which was used to feed the cattle.

1861: Texas was one of several Southern states that relied on enslaved Black people to raise crops and do other important jobs. Many Southern slaveowners feared President Abraham Lincoln would end slavery. Texas and ten other states that allowed slavery created a new nation, the Confederate States. When those states split from the Union, the Civil War began.

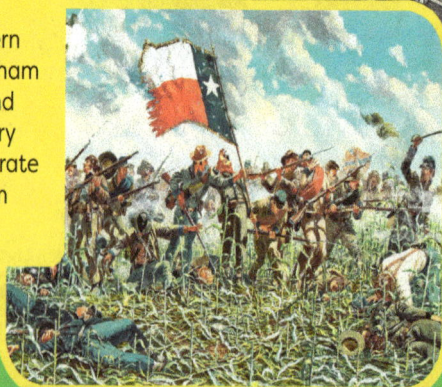

1865: The Civil War ended, as the North defeated the South. Texas's enslaved people won their freedom on a day called Juneteenth. Even so, new laws made it hard for Black people across the state to find jobs or vote.

1870s: Work began on the Houston Ship Channel, to make it easier to move goods into and out of the city. Houston also became a center for railroad travel. By 1891, it had eleven different railways.

The city was growing, but still had only about 10,000 people when this map was made in 1873.

1900: A powerful hurricane destroyed large parts of Galveston, about 50 miles from Houston, and killed at least 6,000 people. (It remains the deadliest natural disaster in American history.) After the Great Storm, Houston became the most important port in Texas.

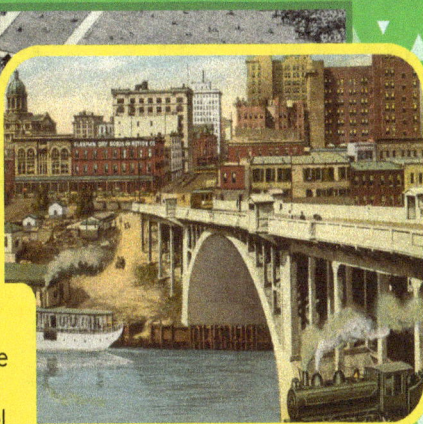

Houston 19

HISTORY: Boom Time!

The 20th century saw Houston turn into the major city it is today.

1901: Oil was discovered near Beaumont, about 80 miles from Houston. The area became the center of a new oil industry. Demand for oil grew to power cars and factories. The city was on its way to becoming "the energy capital of the world."

1917: During World War I, Black and white soldiers trained at Camp Logan. But the area at that time was deeply segregated. When local police arrested a few black soldiers, a fight broke out, and 16 people died. Tragedy struck again a year later, when Camp Logan was the site of a large flu outbreak.

1920s: Refineries, which turn oil into gasoline and other products, were built along the Houston Ship Channel to make transporting the "black gold" easier.

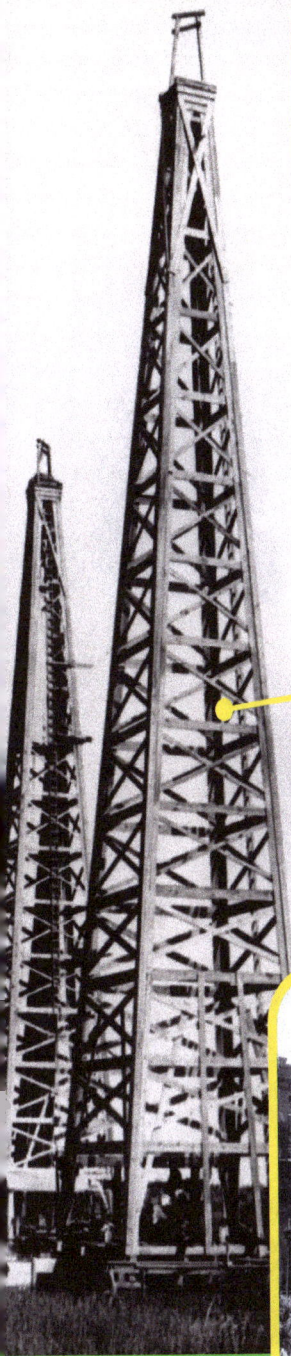

1929: The Great Depression began. Through the 1930s, millions of people lost their jobs and their homes. Thanks to its oil industry, Houston wasn't as hard hit as other cities. Banks across the United States went out of business, but none in Houston did. But in Houston and across Texas, Mexican immigrants were forced to return to their home country. The U.S. government wanted to give their jobs to white workers.

Oil derricks grew like a forest all across east Texas.

1941: The United States entered World War II. Houston did its part, as one of its shipbuilding companies made more than 200 ships. Along with many other companies nationwide, Hughes Tools hired women to make weapons and gear in their factories, to fill the jobs of men who'd gone off to war.

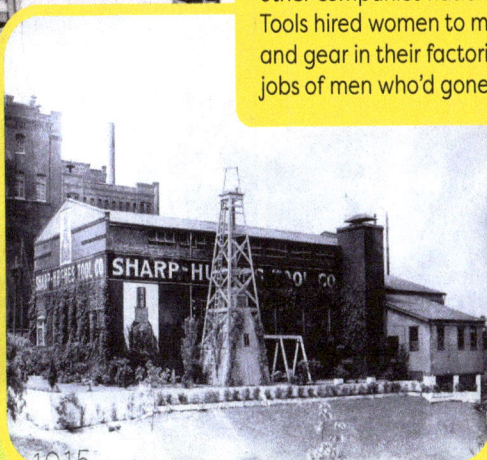

SHARP-HUGHES TOOL CO

1915

HISTORY: 60s and 70s

1965: Dome sweet dome—the Houston Astrodome opened. It was the world's first air-conditioned stadium and was home to the city's baseball team, the Astros. The field was covered with fake grass called Astroturf. Other events held there included basketball games, boxing matches, and concerts. The Astrodome closed in 1999.

1970s: More than 200 major companies, many connected to the oil and gas industries, opened offices in Houston.

1961: Houston became Space City when NASA opened its Manned Space Center. At the center, scientists and engineers tracked the space flights that led to the landing of the first people on the moon in 1969. Today, the center is named the Lyndon B. Johnson Space Center, after the Texas-born 36th president of the United States.

FAST FACT

The first spaceflight tracked by Houston was in 1959. Houston also tracked all six Apollo moon missions.

Grasshopper pumps like these replaced most of the derrricks.

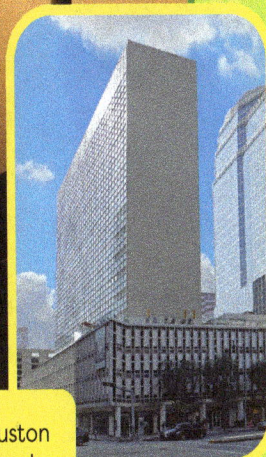

1960s: Dr. Michael DeBakey of Houston Methodist Hospital performed several heart surgeries that had never been done before, including heart bypass and the first heart-lung transplant.

HOUSTON TODAY

Houston has earned a spot as one of the most important cities in the United States. And it's not just because of its size. Here are some of the things Houston is best known for today.

Chemicals: Many chemicals are made from oil—gasoline, gels, lubricants, plastics, and much more—so it's no surprise that some big chemical companies call Houston home. How big? Their sales each year reach tens of billions of dollars! The companies include BASF, DowDuPont, and Exxon Mobil Chemical.

FAST FACT
Houston is the biggest oil-producing city in the US. If Texas were a country, it would be #6 in the world in oil production.

Energy: Major companies that produce oil and natural gas or build the equipment to do so are based in or near Houston. They include Phillips 66, Shell, BP, and Halliburton.

BY THE NUMBERS

Each year, the docs at the
Texas Medical Center:

• Perform more than 180,000 surgeries
• See more than 750,000 emergency
room patients
• Deliver more than 25,000 babies

Medicine: The Texas Medical Center in Houston is the largest medical center in the world! It includes the world's largest hospital for children and the largest hospital for cancer patients. The center's doctors also do important research. More than 106,000 people work at the center.

People from Houston

Here's a quick look at some of the people who helped make Houston what it is today.

Jack Yates

Jack Yates was born into slavery in Virginia and was forced to come to Texas by his enslaver. When Yates was liberated in 1865, he moved to Houston as a free man. Despite these terrible beginnings, Yates became a leader in the African American community. He became a minister, started a school for African American children, and helped his community buy Emancipation Park (see page 27). His home was later moved to Sam Houston Park and is open to the public.

Ima Hogg

Miss Hogg's parents must have had a strange sense of humor. But what Ima did for Houston is no laughing matter. Ima and her brothers struck it rich in 1919 when oil was found on family land. Hogg then used some of her money to start the Houston Symphony Orchestra and rebuild some of the city's old buildings. Hogg was also an art collector. She donated her art and magnificent mansion to Houston's Museum of Fine Arts.

Jesse Jones

If one person helped make Houston a bustling big city, it was Jesse Jones. Born in Tennessee, he arrived in Houston in 1898 and made a fortune in real estate and banking. He built the city's first skyscrapers—just ten stories or so back then—then kept on building. Jones also led the effort to keep Texas banks open during the Great Depression in the 1930s. It's no wonder that he was sometimes called "Mr. Houston."

Mario E. Figueroa

That name might not mean much to many Houstonians. They know Mario better as GONZO247. The Houston native's murals can be found all over walls in the city, as well as galleries, hotels, and city buildings. He pioneered graffiti and street art as important alternative art in Houston. GONZO247 helps people to see that street art is just as important as fine art.

HOUSTON for Everyone

Houston is known for is its mix of people from different backgrounds. It's one of the most diverse big cities in the United States. Who are these diverse Houstonians? Let's take a look.

Latinx to the Max

Since Texas was once part of Mexico, it's not surprising that so many Houstonians have roots there or are from there. Some are people whose families settled in the region generations ago, while others are more recent arrivals from Mexico, Central America, or other Spanish-speaking countries. By 2020, Latinx people made up the largest percentage of the population in Houston and surrounding towns at 45 percent. Latinx Houstonians are senators, judges, symphony directors, professors, and more. Ellen Ochoa was the first female astronaut in space!

Every year from September 15 to October 15 Houston celebrates Hispanic Heritage Month showcasing all that the Latinx community has done to help make Houston a world-class city full of art, innovation, and delicious food.

The Black Influence in Houston

White settlers in Texas were often enslavers who forced enslaved people to work for them. In 1865, after the end of the Civil War, enslaved people were finally liberated and many moved to Houston. In 1872 a group of freedmen raised $1000 to buy and build Emancipation Park (*emancipation* means "the freeing of enslaved people") to host celebrations of Juneteenth. Over time, though, white city leaders passed laws and practices that decided where African American Houstonians could live, go to school, eat, and play. They did not allow Black families to live in white neighborhoods or go to school with white children. This practice of separating people based on their race is called segregation and is harmful.

Despite all of this poor treatment, African American Houstonians have persevered. They have made important contributions to the history of the city. Many Houston museums showcase that history, including the Buffalo Soldier National Museum. Buffalo Soldiers were responsible for protecting western settlers and even fought in wars. Native Americans gave them that name in respect for their bravery, just like buffaloes.

FAST FACT

The national holiday Juneteenth began in Texas. June 19 celebrates the day in 1865 when enslaved people in Texas learned that they had been liberated. It had taken two years for the Union Army to reach them with the news.

HOUSTON for Everyone

Seeking A New Life

Houston has a large Asian population—more than 1.5 million people from many Asian countries. When the Vietnam War ended in 1975, people from Vietnam and its neighboring countries, such as Cambodia and Laos, came to Texas. Many of them settled in Houston. The first Vietnamese to arrive often lived and worked in one area that's now known as Little Saigon (Saigon was renamed Ho Chi Minh City in 1975). Today, Houston has one of the largest Vietnamese-American communities in the country.

People from other Asian nations, such as India and China, have also settled in Houston. The first Chinese immigrants came in 1870 and worked to build railroads. Today, many students come from Asian countries, especially India, to study at one of the many universities in Houston. Asiatown is a vibrant part of Houston that celebrates Asian culture and features many Asian-owned businesses and restaurants.

Germans in Houston

Since Houston was founded, people from all over Europe have made Houston their home. People from Germany, though, had a special fondness for the city and the region around it. Most worked as farmers. Some settled in a part of the Houston area known today as Tomball. Some schools and businesses there have German names.

Today Tomball honors its German roots with two festivals. One is a Christmas market. It's modeled on the ones held in Germany. People can buy handmade gifts. The other festival features German music, food, and people dressed in clothing worn back in the "old country." You don't have to be German to enjoy the festivals. The folks in Tomball say *Wilkommen*, or welcome, to everyone!

High Heat and Big Storms
Houston Climate and Weather

When some people think of Houston, they think of heat. High heat, for months on end. In August, the average daily high temperature is over 94 degrees! And don't forget the humidity. That refers to how much water is in the air. High humidity is what makes you really sticky on a hot day.

The heat and humidity are part of Houston's climate. They're so intense, the city has six miles of air-conditioned tunnels that connect many downtown buildings. That way, people can move around and stay cool. You could say the invention of air conditioning made Houston what it is today. Few folks would want to live there if they didn't have a way to beat the heat!

If the heat wasn't bad enough, Houston has also seen some powerful hurricanes storm ashore. The hurricanes usually form over the Atlantic Ocean and then blow in from the Gulf of Mexico. Houston rarely gets a direct hit, but the storms still bring plenty of rain. In 2017, Hurricane Harvey dumped 29 inches of rain in two days! The water led to floods across the city. Even without hurricanes, the city gets lots of rain. On average, rain falls 180 days a year.

FAST FACTS

FAST FACTS
Climate means what the weather is like over long periods of time each year. Weather means what it's like outside right now!

When to Visit

December through February are the coolest months in Houston. But cool doesn't mean cold—average daytime temps are still in the 60s. The city can even get some snow in the winter, though it doesn't happen every year. The best time to visit may be spring, before it gets too hot and when flowers start to bloom.

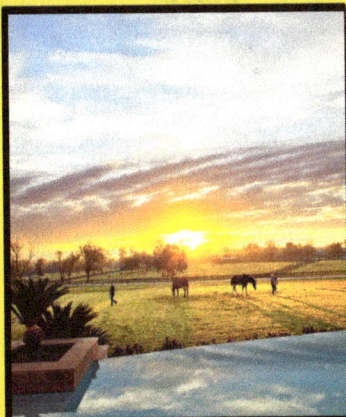

Hey! I'm from Houston!

Jim Parsons

As an actor, Jim Parsons made a big bang on television. Playing Sheldon Cooper, Parsons was one of the stars of the hit comedy, *The Big Bang Theory*. Parsons was born in Houston in 1973 and got the acting bug at an early age, appearing in plays. For his role as Sheldon, he won several awards. Parsons still acts on stage, and also in films.

While going to a segregated school in Houston, young Barbara Jordan became interested in becoming a lawyer. She wanted to end practices that denied Black Americans equal treatment. Jordan became a lawyer, and then she was elected to the U.S. House of Representatives. She was the first black woman from the South to serve in the House.

Barbara Jordan

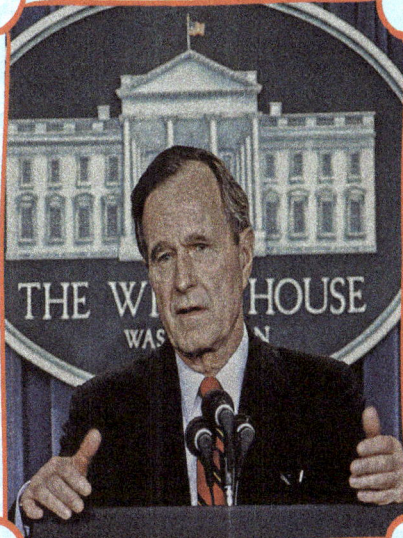
George H.W. Bush

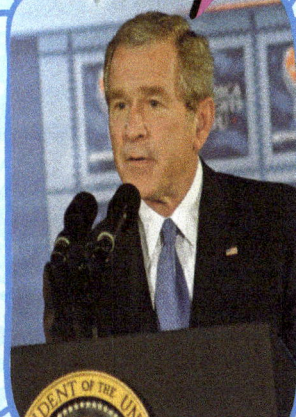
George W. Bush

George H.W. and George W. Bush

Houston is the former home of not one, but two, U.S. presidents. George H. W. Bush moved with wife Barbara and their children to Houston in 1959. Bush entered politics a few years later. He served as president from 1989 to 1993 and then returned to Houston. His son George spent only a few years in the city before heading east to go to college.

The younger Bush was the governor of Texas before becoming president in 2001. He served until 2009.

Things to see in Houston

Tourist time! If you're a Houstonian, you (probably) know all about these places. But if you're visiting, here are the sights to see.

Johnson Space Center Houston

Houston, we have no problem . . . telling everyone about NASA's mission to the moon (and more)! The Johnson Space Center is a leading center for space research and exploration. One part of it—Space Center Houston—is open to the public, and you should go visit! What can you see?

In the Starship Gallery, blast off into history as you marvel at the Apollo 16 spaceship that carried the last astronauts to land on the moon—so far. You'll see rocks collected on the moon. There's also a space "car," called a lunar rover. And you can see space suits worn by real astronauts (left).

In the Mission Mars section, learn what it will take to live on the "Red Planet." Other sights include an exhibit on the International Space Station and a visit to the Mission Control Center that was used in the 1960s to guide trips to the moon!

Things to see in Houston

Honoring Heroes

Texas and Houston history might be a lot different if Texans hadn't defeated the Mexican Army along the San Jacinto River in 1836. Learn all about the key battle at San Jacinto Battleground Historic State Park. Don't miss the elevator ride to the top of the park's 570-foot tower. That height includes the 34-foot-tall star that sits on top. The star refers to Texas's nickname—the Lone Star State.

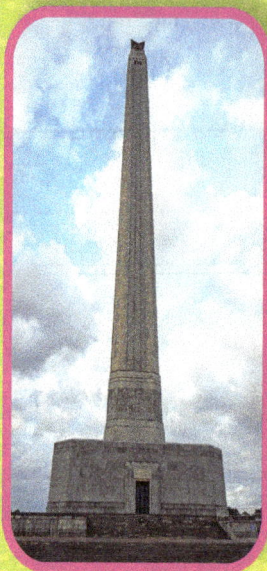

The Orange Show

Every city has at least one odd attraction. For Houston, this one might take the cake—an orange cake, of course. The Orange Show honors that thick-skinned fruit. Jeff McKissack was a mail carrier who loved oranges. He began building this spot to honor his favorite fruit and worked on it until his death in 1980. McKissack made most of it out of old items he found along the road or in junkyards. Inside, he put artwork about oranges. After McKissack died, some Houston art lovers bought the site to make sure everyone could see his love for that fruit. Today it's called The Orange Show Center for Visionary Art.

Tunnel Tour

Remember those tunnels below the streets that help keep folks cool during the sweltering heat? You can explore them as part of a tour. The first tunnels opened during the 1930s, and now Houston's downtown has the largest system of pedestrian tunnels in the country. The tour takes you past restaurants and shops, and you can poke your head above ground to see some of the big buildings linked by the tunnels.

Houston Arboretum and Nature Center

For wildlife of a different kind, head to the Houston Arboretum and Nature Center. An arboretum displays trees and plants so people can learn all about them. With its nature center, Houston's arboretum also gives visitors the scoop on local birds, insects, and animals. The center has programs just for kids, so they can see if they might like to be an animal scientist someday.

Things to see in Houston

Rice University

Inside the buildings here students come from all around the world to learn. Outside, Rice University has a beautiful setting. It has sculptures scattered around, and a stunning building called the Skyspace (right). It was built to hold concerts, but it's a work of art, too. The upper part has no walls, and the roof has a large hole in it so guests can see the sky. At sunrise and sunset, Skyspace projects colored lights onto the roof.

Ship Channel Boat Tours

Thanks to its Ship Channel, Houston is one of the world's largest ports. That's pretty impressive, since the city is 50 miles away from the Gulf of Mexico! You can see some of the ships and learn more about the channel on a free 90-minue tour. Visitors ride on a boat named for Sam Houston and learn about work in the port.

Discovery Green

One of Houston's newest outdoor spaces is Discovery Green. It opened in the heart of the city in 2008. It hosts concerts and other events and is filled with art. One piece is called Mistree. It sort of looks like a steel tree, and it rains down misty water. It's a perfect place to cool off on a hot Houston day. Dogs can get in on the fun at Discovery Green, too. It has special areas set aside where canines can run and play together.

Listen Up!

Two of the coolest spots at Discovery Green make up the Listening Vessel. These two curved, stone sculptures are 70 feet apart. Two people sit inside them across from each other. When one person whispers something, the other person can hear it. The round shape of the vessels helps those faint sounds travel far.

Cockrell Butterfly Center

Under a huge glass dome you can visit with thousands of flittering and flapping butterflies. A huge waterfall and tons of bright green plants make it feel like you're in a rain forest. Stand still and see if you can get the butterflies to land on your head! The center is near the Museum of Natural Science (see page 52).

One Big Park!

Memorial Park is home to an arboretum and nature center—and a whole lot more! A wealthy Houston family called the Hoggs bought the land for the park. It had been the site of Camp Logan, where soldiers trained for World War I. Four million people come to the park every year to exercise, play sports, and enjoy nature. The park has jogging trails, ball fields, a swimming pool, and its own golf course. There are even courts where you can play croquet.

GETTING AROUND

HOUSTON

Airports: How can you tell that Houston is a really important city? It has two airports! The largest is named for the first President Bush. Folks can fly there directly from more than 170 cities around the world.

Light Rail: Once visitors reach Houston, they can get around in several ways. Since the city covers so much ground, most people prefer to drive. But Houston also has a light rail system. That means the trains aren't as big or fast as the trains that travel between cities. Three different rail lines connect most of the city's hot spots. Houston once had street cars. The first ones were pulled by mules! Electricity powered the cars from the 1890s through the 1940. The current rail system opened in 2004.

MetroRapid: One vehicle that speeds around Houston might have you scratching your head. Is it a bus? Is it light rail? No, it's MetroRapid! It looks like a long bus split into two sections. But unlike a bus, it has its own lane. So, it doesn't have to compete with cars. It also has its own special stations, like the light rail system.

Bicycles: Since cars are such a huge part of life in Houston, cycling on crowded city streets can be challenging. The city makes cycling safer with a series of bike paths and trails. Many miles of paved trails run next to streets and bayous. The city is also building bike lanes on some streets. The goal is to one day have 700 miles of bike lanes.

IT'S OFFICIAL!

Cities like to name "official" things. That basically just means that lots of people who live there like something! Here are some of Houston's "official" city things.

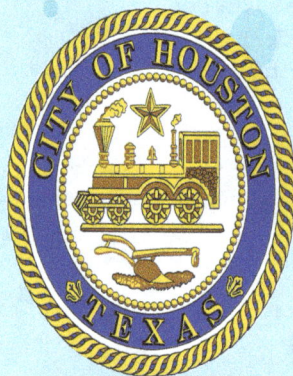

OFFICIAL CITY FLAG:
The flag features the official seal of Houston, which dates to 1840. The seal has a "lone star" that represents Texas. The steam engine is a sign that Houston wanted to be a city of progress. And the plow salutes the farmers who settled in the region.

OFFICIAL CITY BIRD:
Yellow-crowned Night Heron

OFFICIAL CITY SONG:

Houston's song doesn't have a catchy name—it's just called the Municipal Song. Municipal refers to a city or its government. The song was written in 1915 and then pretty much forgotten. In 2016, a local singing group recorded the song. It was probably the first time most Houstonians even knew their city had an official song!

OFFICIAL TEXAS STATE STUFF
(this is just some of them—the state has more than 50 official things!)

Amphibian: Texas toad
Bird: Mockingbird
Fish: Guadalupe bass
Folk Dance: Square dance
Footwear: Cowboy boot
Insect: Monarch butterfly
Mammal, small: Armadillo
Musical instrument: Guitar
Pie: Pecan Pie
Sport: Rodeo

Smither Park: This park features mosaic art made by local residents. In mosaics, tiny pieces of tile are glued down in patterns and shapes. At Smither Park, more than tiles are used. Some of its mosaics are made from items people have found lying around, like broken dinner plates and glass.

Art in Houston

Art can be found outdoors all over Houston, from giant presidents' heads to an eight-foot snowman to a collection of wild metal birds!

"Mount Rush Hour" American Statesmanship Park: South Dakota has its Mount Rushmore. It has gigantic stone sculptures of four U.S. presidents. Well, Houston has American Statesmanship Park. This park features the heads of two big Texans: Stephen Austin, who brought American settlers to the state, and Sam Houston. Joining them are Presidents Abe Lincoln and George Washington. Each head—and a little bit of chest—is 16 feet tall. Locals call it Mount Rush Hour. That's because they can see the four statues as they drive to and from work.

Where can you see a giant spider, an enormous armadillo, and other larger-than-life critters? At the **Eclectic Menagerie Park**. Eclectic refers to a wide variety of things, and this art park fits the bill. It's built on land owned by a company that sells metal pipes. The metal sculptures (sort of like this one) are all the work of Houstonian Ron Lee. All in all, there are more than two dozen of them at the park.

Art in Houston

Most of Houston's best-known museums are in the city's Museum District. That one small area is packed with 19 museums! Here's a look at a few.

Museum of Fine Arts, Houston
You can get a history of world art in this museum. It's filled with almost 70,000 different art objects. They include paintings, sculptures, jewelry, and clothing. Some items are up to 4,000 years old! See Impressionist masters, American paintings, and contemporary arts from Texas and the Southwest.

ROSBARRIE SETTEGAST
LANGDON · FOUNTAIN

Houston Center for Contemporary Craft
Some folks are naturally crafty—that means they know how to make crafts. They might work with clay, glass, wood, or "found" materials—things other people have thrown away. The museum's visitors can see artists at work and talk to them about their crafts.

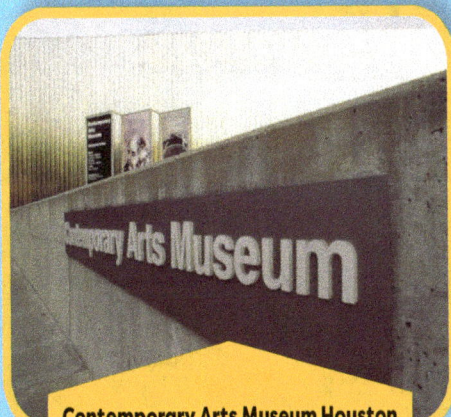

Contemporary Arts Museum Houston

Contemporary refers to art made in recent times—right up to today! This museum doesn't buy art to display. Instead, it invites different artists to show their work in exhibits that are always changing. The artists are local, national, or from around the world. Some folks say the museum's steel building is a work of art itself.

Houston Center for Photography

This is more than just a place to see exhibits by famous photographers from around the world. Locals can take classes in photography and learn how to use film and digital cameras.

Four-Wheeled Wonders

If you think cars are cool, leave the Museum District and cruise over to the Art Car Museum. It features cars that have been decorated in all sorts of ways. Some have been painted, while others are covered with jewels and beads—or even plastic alligators! Some of the cars roll through Houston during the annual Art Car Parade.

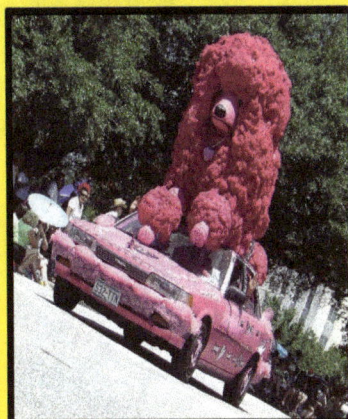

Other Great Houston Museums

Museums are great for more than art, of course. Houston has something for just about everyone!

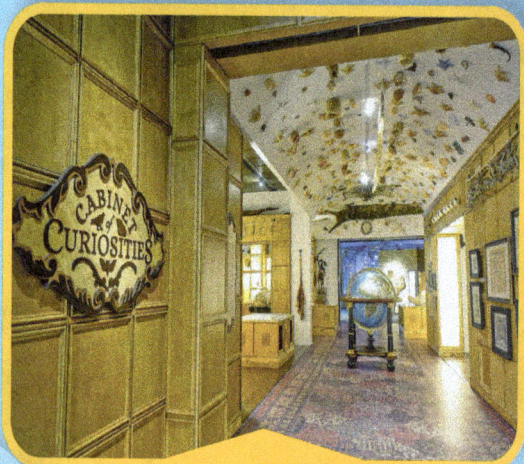

Houston Children's Museum

Kids who want a museum just for them love this place. There's the Genius Station, where they can ask science teachers questions. Visitors can also help perform experiments. The SECRETS Spy Game turns you into a super sleuth trying to crack secret codes and solve puzzles. You can even explore a foreign country without leaving the museum. The exhibit called Heart and Seoul shows how kids live in South Korea and its capital city.

Houston Museum of Natural Science

Make no bones about it—this museum is perfect for dinosaur lovers. They can see skeletons of triceratops and other ancient beasts. But there's more in store here than just old bones. The museum also has gems and minerals and exhibits on chemistry and energy. It also has a "Cabinet of Curiosities." Here, you can check out stuffed critters, animal bones, and other items from the natural world. It's definitely kid-friendly, as you can touch many of the items.

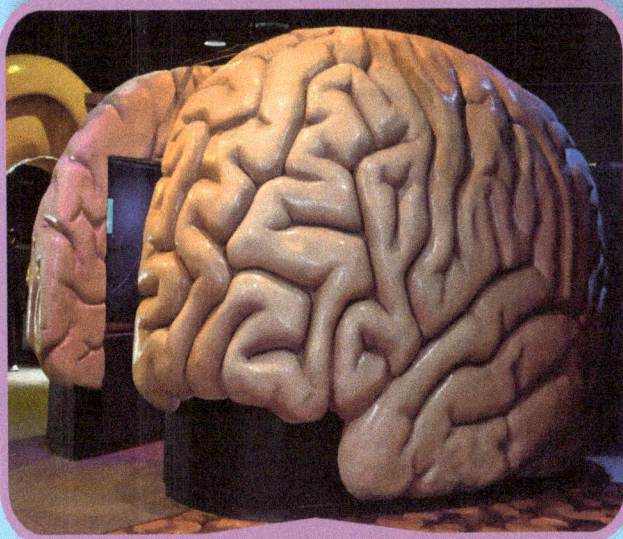

Health Museum

Houston is known for its hospitals and medical research. To learn more about the human body and how to keep it healthy, head to this museum. You can walk through a model of the brain or learn about our sight with an enormous eyeball. In the Cell Lab, you dress like a real scientist at work. That's because you get to carry out experiments that teach you more about the body.

Project Row Houses

Art, history, and community come together in this collection of restored houses in the Third Ward. Artists present their visions, community events are held, and music is performed. There's something for everyone!

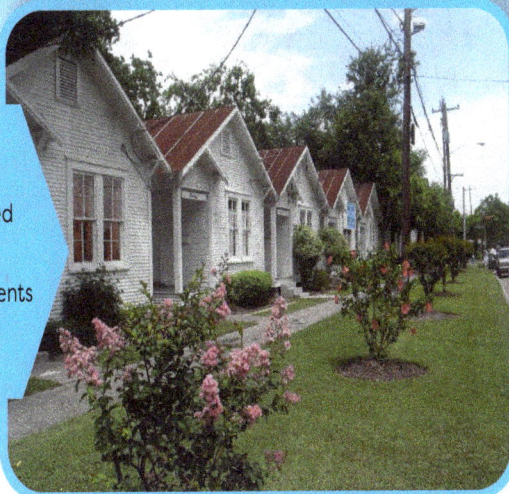

See the World in Houston

Explore more of Houston's diversity in these museums. They look at the history and culture of people from around the world who have helped shape the city.

Czech Center Museum Houston ➤ People from the Czech Republic and Slovakia were among the people who first settled in the Houston region. Here, you can learn about their history and the art and stories they brought with them to America.

◄ **Asia Society Texas Center** The center teaches about the people and countries of Asia. Recent exhibits have featured artists from Bangladesh, China, and Tibet.

Houston Museum of African American Culture ▼

The museum displays art by Black Americans and Africans. This museum has art and wisdom from both African Americans and people from the African Diaspora. It has exhibits and events to help shape our future together.

HMAAC

◄ **Institute of Hispanic Culture Houston** It's not really a museum, but it is a center for art created by artists from many Latinx nations. The institute displays art, holds concerts, and raises money for students. That money helps young Latinx students in Houston study art.

Live! On Stage!

Houston has talented performers who entertain audiences across the city. Here's just some of the performing art you can see.

Both the **Houston Ballet** and the **Houston Grand Opera** call the Wortham Theater Center their home. The center has two theaters. The smaller one is often used by visiting opera companies.

Dancers! Check out the Houston Ballet—with 59 dancers it's the fifth-largest in the country.

Plays come to life at the **Alley Theater**. It has two stages, with the largest theater able to hold almost 800 people.

Rock on at the **White Oak Music Hall**, which offers live music on one outdoor and two indoor stages.

How to Talk Houston

Some words and sayings only make sense to the people who live in a particular place or city. Here are some things you might hear folks in Houston say.

INSIDE OR OUTSIDE THE LOOP

A highway called Interstate 610 forms a big loop around the center of Houston. People and places are located either inside or outside the Loop.

CLUTCH CITY

This is one of Houston's nicknames, though it's not as common as Space City or H-town. In sports, being clutch means making a big play when it really counts. The Houston Rockets were very clutch when they won their two basketball championships during the 1990s.

Trill

If you call someone or something trill, that's a good thing. It means they're true or real. The word was first used by rappers in the Houston area.

EaDo

Heading to a pro soccer game or a hot new restaurant? Then you're going to end up in the Houston neighborhood called EaDo. That's short for East Downtown. Not too long ago, the area was filled with old warehouses. Now, it's where many people want to live.

SLAB

No, not like a slab of concrete. SLAB stands for "slow, low, and banging," and describes a very cool car.

Y'all

Ok, this one works all over Texas. It's short for "you all," and it can refer to one person, or a whole group of them.

HOUSTON: It's Weird!

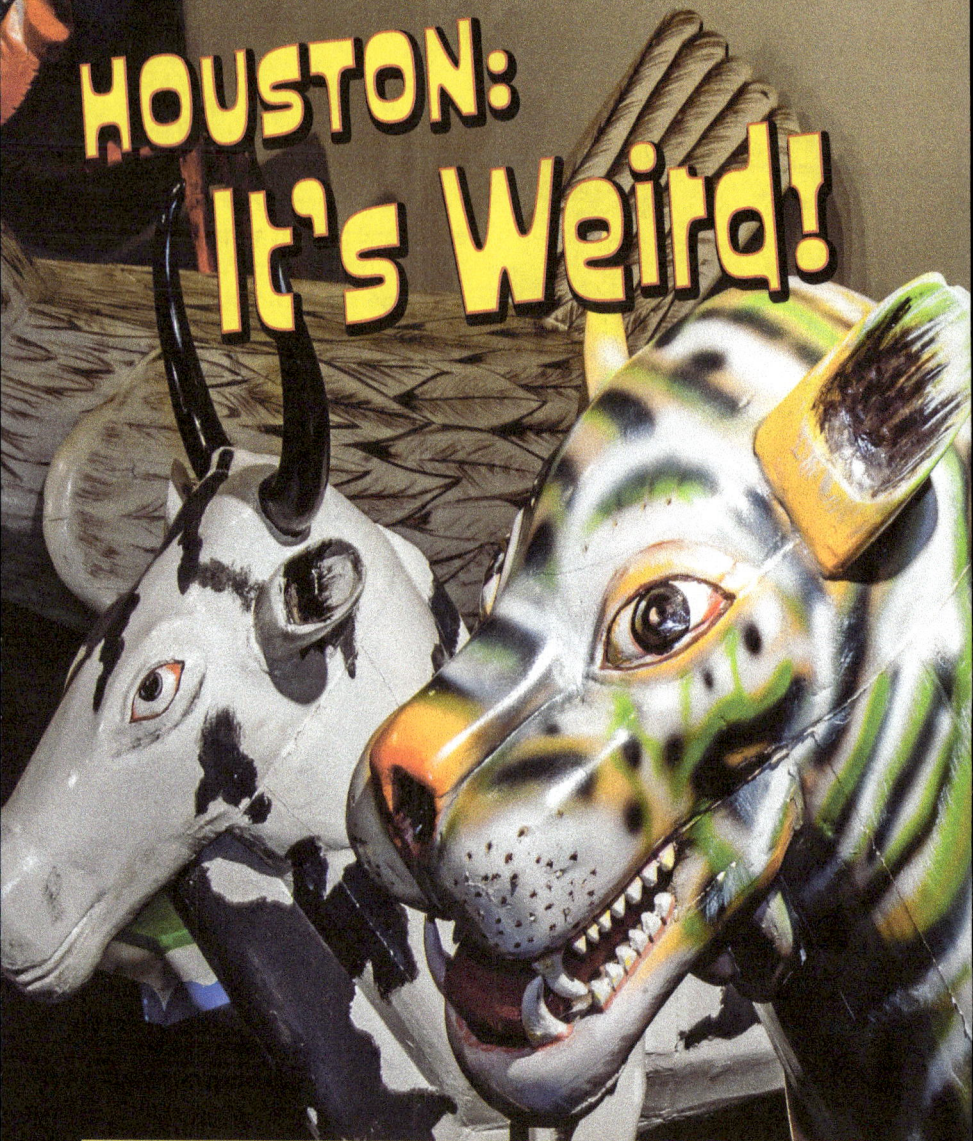

Dig Deep

Houston can claim to have the world's only museum that explores the history of funerals. The National Museum of Funeral History shows how people in other countries bury their dead. There are also plenty of coffins on display. You can see hearses too—those are the cars that carry the dead to their final resting spot. One exhibit features the hearse used for the funerals of two U.S. presidents.

Keep It Clean!

Wash away the grime from the family car at Buc-ee's Car Wash. It's in Katy, just west of Houston. At 255 feet, it's the longest car wash in the world. It takes five minutes for cars to roll past the 25 sets of brushes.

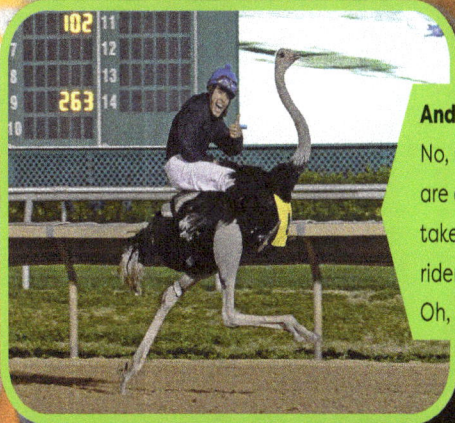

And They're Off!?

No, not horses. In this case, "they" are camels and ostriches. They take a turn around the track, with riders, at Sam Houston Race Park. Oh, and horses race there, too.

The Red Button!

Go ahead, push it. The city wants you to press the button on one of the bridges that crosses Buffalo Bayou. The button doesn't say what it's for. But when you push it, the bayou lets out a big "burp." The burping moves the water in the bayou, which keeps it from getting stinky.

What People Do
IN HOUSTON

Along with the 2.3 million people who live in Houston, another 5 million or so live in the metro area. Here's how some of those folks make a living.

Energy: Houston isn't called the energy capital of the world for nothing! Most people know the big energy companies like Shell and BP. But the area also has several thousand smaller companies that take oil and gas out of the ground and turn it into fuel you can use.

Life Sciences: Companies that research health issues and make medicines are big in Houston. The major medicine makers include Bayer and Novartis.

Food: When you eat in a restaurant, there's a good chance your food has Houston roots. Sysco provides food to restaurants around the world, and its headquarters are in Houston.

Petrochemicals: Stuff made from oil is called petrochemicals. Houston is the center of that industry in the United States. The major companies include ExxonMobil, DowDuPont, and BP. Their petrochemicals are used to make plastics, furniture, electronics, and more.

Shipping: Houston's port is one hopping place. It's the busiest port in the country, based on the total weight of all the international goods that move in and out.

Beyoncé

Born in Houston: September 4, 1981

This Houston native, known as "Queen Bey" to her fans, is one of the world's most successful entertainers. She's a singer, dancer, actor, successful businesswoman, mom—seems like there's not much she can't do! Beyoncé sometimes mentions places in Houston in her songs, like the Third Ward, where she grew up. She's also filmed music videos in her hometown.

George Foreman

Born near Houston: January 10, 1945

You might know George's name from the little grill he sells. But before he got into cooking, he was one of the world's best boxers. He was the world's heavyweight champion two different times. The second time, he was 45 years old—the oldest heavyweight champ ever! Foreman's family moved to Houston's Sixth Ward when he was still a baby. After he was done boxing, George opened a gym and community center in Houston.

Eat the Houston Way

Dishes from Mexico, Vietnam, and other countries are often on the menu in Houston. So is Cajun cooking, which has its roots in nearby Louisiana. Here's a sample of some excellent Houston eats.

What We Eat From Texas

Beef * Chicken * Milk
Rice * Wheat * Peanuts

Tex-Mex!

Blend food from Texas and Mexico and you get Tex-Mex. Popular dishes include enchiladas, tacos, and tamales. Fiery chile peppers give the sauces some heat.

Not Your Usual Sandwich

Vietnamese immigrants brought a special sandwich to Houston. A báhn mi has meat and veggies packed inside French bread.

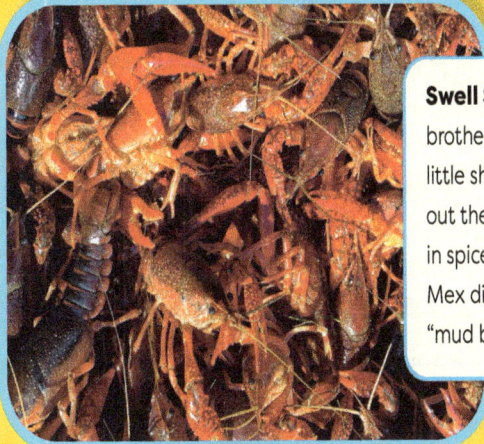

Swell Shellfish

Crawfish look like lobsters' kid brothers or sisters. Houstonians gobble up these little shellfish in lots of ways. Most popular is to pick out the meat after the crawfish have been boiled in spiced water. The meat can also turn up in Tex-Mex dishes. Some Vietnamese cooks toss the boiled "mud bug" in melted butter and more spices.

Barbecue for You

Lots of Houston's restaurants claim to have the best barbecue. Some secrets to cooking meat this way? Find the right rub, or mix of spices, that covers the meat. Cook it for a *loooong* time in a smoker. Top it with just the right sauce—a little tangy, a little sweet.

Taking the Field!

Houston is home to some top-notch pro sports teams. Cheer them on!

nrg stadium

Andre Johnson

HOUSTON TEXANS

Joined the National Football League in 2002.

Cool Stuff: Since 2011, have won the NFC South division six times, but have never advanced to the Super Bowl.

Big Names: Andre Johnson, Matt Schaub, J. J. Watt, DeShaun Watson

Home: NRG Stadium

FAST FACTS
Houston's first NFL team was called the Oilers. They moved to Nashville for the 1997 season. Today the team is known as the Tennessee Titans.

HOUSTON ASTROS

Joined Major League Baseball in 1962. First called the Colt 45s, the Astros were once in the National League. Now, they're in the American League.

Cool Stuff: Have been in the World Series three times and won it in 2017.

Big Names: Nolan Ryan, Jeff Bagwell, Craig Biggio, José Altuve, J. R. Richard, Joe Niekro

Home: Minute Maid Park

José Altuve

HOUSTON ROCKETS

Joined the National Basketball Association in 1967. The team played its first four seasons in San Diego before coming to Houston in 1971.

Cool Stuff: Won the NBA championship in 1994 and 1995

Big Names Hakeem Olajuwon, James Harden, Calvin Murphy, Rudy Tomjanovich, Yao Ming

Home: Toyota Center

Hakeem Olajuwon

HOUSTON DYNAMO FC

Joined Major League Soccer in 1996.

The team was originally based in San Diego. It first played in Houston in 2006.

Won MLS Cup in 2006 and 2007. Won the U.S. Open Cup in 2018. That competition includes teams from several different leagues.

Plays in the Texas Derby each year against the MLS team from Dallas.

Big Names: Brian Ching, Brad Davis, DaMarcus Beasley

Home: BBVA Stadium

Houston once had a Women's National Basketball Association team called the Comets. Starting in 1997, the Comets won four league championships in a row! The team shut down in 2008.

HOUSTON DASH

Joined the National Women's Soccer League in 2014.

In 2020, won the league's first Challenge Cup.

Team owners include boxing great Oscar de la Hoya and basketball star James Harden.

Big Names: Kealia Ohai, Carli Lloyd, Sofia Huerta

Home: BBVA Stadium

The city once had a pro hockey team, too. The Aeros played in the World Hockey Association from 1972 to 1978. Its star was one of the greatest hockey players of all time, Gordie Howe.

Other Sports!

How do Houstonians stay active? Here are some of the ways they get their hearts pumping!

Houston's parks are filled with trails for **hiking** and **cycling**. Buffalo Bayou Park is a popular spot, especially for bicycles. So are the trails in Hermann and Memorial Parks. If you ride on smaller wheels, Buffalo Bayou has its own skate park for **skateboarding**.

If you prefer to get your exercise on the water, Buffalo Bayou fits the bill. Folks use it for **kayaking** and **canoeing**. If they don't have their own boat, they can rent one at the park. Several lakes just outside Houston provide more spots where you can paddle around.

You can get into the swing of things at seven city-owned **golf courses**. The one at Memorial Park even has its own golf museum.

Surf's up! Well, not in Houston itself, but the shores of the Gulf of Mexico are just a short drive away. Several spots near Galveston have good waves for surfing, stand-up paddling and other **water sports**.

COLLEGE TOWN

Houstonians can pursue a college degree at several schools. Here are some of the biggies:

UNIVERSITY OF HOUSTON

Founded 1927
Students: 47,000
Popular majors: business, marketing, engineering, psychology, biological and biomedical sciences
Fast Fact: During the 1980s, the men's basketball team twice reached the finals of the NCAA championship.

TEXAS SOUTHERN UNIVERSITY

Founded 1927
Students: 9,700
Popular majors: banking and financial support services, biology/biological sciences, business administration and management, criminal justice/law enforcement administration.
Fast Fact: Barbara Jordan (see page 34) graduated from this historically Black university (HBU).

RICE UNIVERSITY

Founded 1912
Students: 7,700
Popular majors: computer and information sciences, mechanical engineering, economics, and biochemistry.
Fast Fact: Rice is considered one of the best private schools in the country.

UNIVERSITY OF TEXAS HEALTH SCIENCE CENTER

Founded 1972
Students: 4,300
Popular majors: nursing, medicine, biomedical informatics, biomedical sciences, dentistry, and public health.
Fast Fact: The science center in Houston is the sixth-largest medical school in the United States.

HOUSTON BAPTIST UNIVERSITY

Founded 1962
Students: 4,000
Popular majors: health professions, business, marketing, biological/biomedical sciences; fitness studies; and psychology.
Fast Fact: The school has a museum that features rare bibles from around the world.

Rice University's main building

LOL!

Houston Funnies!

Go ahead and laugh at Houston—its people won't mind! Here are some riddles to tickle your funny bone.

Why are NASA and Houston like a donut?

They both have a space center.

What do you call a baseball fan who's crazy for Houston?

An Astro-Nut!

Why do so many people go to barbecues in Houston?

So they can "meat" each other.

When did the pot of meat and beans start freezing in Houston?

When they became chili.

Where in Houston can you see the most rockets?

At an NBA basketball game!

Why are there so many elephants in the Houston zoo?

Because they aren't allowed anywhere else.

Which Houston park's name makes you stand next to a bison?

Buffalo "By You" Park.

It's Alive! Wildlife in Houston

Even though Houston is a big, bustling city, plenty of animals call it home. They live in and around the parks and even some suburban neighborhoods. A few of them, such as squirrels and opossums, sometimes try to get into people's homes to build nests.

Raccoons

Coyotes

Foxes

Skunks

Opossums

Armadillos

Armadillos are famous for their "armor"—their body is protected with hard plates. Texas has named them one of its state symbols, and you can spot them around Houston. Some folks complain because the animals dig up their gardens. It might be hard to spot one, though. They sleep up to 16 hours a day and come out mostly at night.

It's Alive! Wildlife in Houston

Local wildlife also finds homes in and around waterways. And when you look up in the sky, you can spot some of the flying critters that live in the region.

Turtles

Snakes and Reptiles

Hognose Snakes
Rat snakes
Wood snakes
Kingsnakes
Copperhead (venomous!)

House geckos
Anoles
Skinks

Herons

Alligators

Ducks

A Helping Hand

Texas Wildlife Rehabilitation Coalition

It can be tough for wild animals trying to live in the city. Houston's growth means less space for some critters. The animals can also get injured or sick. Thanks to helping humans, those animals get medical treatment at the Texas Wildlife Rehabilitation Coalition. The staff there helps the animals get better and then releases them back into the wild.

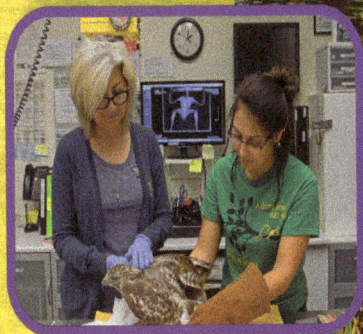

WE SAW IT AT THE ZOO

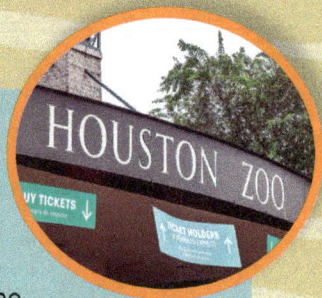

The Houston Zoo was founded way back in 1922. A popular exhibit features some of the wildlife found in the Galapagos Islands. These islands sit off the western coast of South America. Some of the new critters that are part of the exhibit include Humboldt penguins, sea lions, and sharks.

There's plenty to see at the other exhibits, too. The zoo features animals from Africa, like rhinos, chimps, and giraffes. There's also an antelope called the Eastern bongo. Can you beat that?

The zoo also has a touch of Texas wildlife. A nature area features alligators, whooping cranes, and bald eagles. All three are native to Texas.

Bongo

Elephant

Ankole cow

Meerkats

Iguana

Grey-crown crane

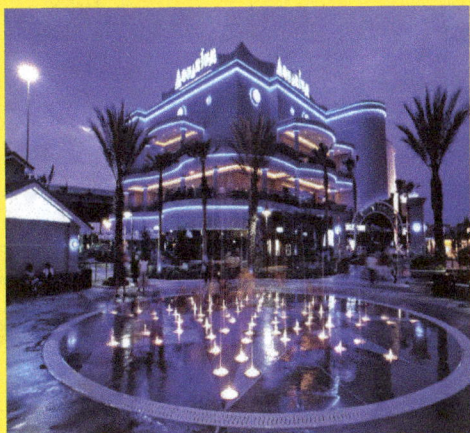

Downtown Aquarium

Houston's aquarium isn't huge, but it's packed with fun. The Texas Bayou exhibit lets you see some of the region's water residents—like alligators! Or you can go on the Shark Voyage. Climb aboard a train that takes you through the center of a tank filled with different types of sharks.

Spooky Sights

Do you believe in ghosts and spirits? Not everyone does . . . but no one knows for sure! Like most cities, Houston has lots of places that people say are haunted.

Diners could get some chills along with their meals at the old **Spaghetti Warehouse** restaurant. The building was built around 1912. Some people say that a worker who died in the building long ago haunts it. His wife joins him, and there might be other ghosts. Some people say the building is one of the most haunted in the country. The restaurant is closed now, but the ghosts might remain!

Mellie Esperson built two buildings in Houston. She liked one of them so much, she never left! The **Esperson Buildings** include one with Mellie's name carved into the stone. She seems to enjoy playing with the elevator especially!

La Carafe was once a bakery. Now it's a bar—and the home of at least one ghost. People have heard the sounds of a child playing on the second floor. Others say a former manager of the bar haunts the place.

Ghosts ahoy! The battleship *Texas* is docked in the Houston Ship Channel, and spirits seem to walk its decks. People have reported feeling "something" (or someone!) walking by them and making noises. One ghost is said to be a sailor who served on the ship.

What's that click-clack sound in the **Julia Ideson Building**? People say it's the toenails of a canine ghost! Petey the dog belonged to Jacob Cramer, who worked in the building. Jacob also lived—and died—in the basement. Both Jacob and Petey are said to roam the halls.

For a time, the **Rice Hotel** was the tallest building in Houston. On the roof was a garden. Today, people say they hear the steps of ghosts dancing on the rooftop. And the sound of rattling doors comes from one room. The most famous guest in it was President John F. Kennedy. He spent time in the room the day before he was shot and killed in Dallas in 1963.

HOUSTON BY THE NUMBERS

Stats and facts and digits galore. Here are some of the numbers that make Houston what it is.

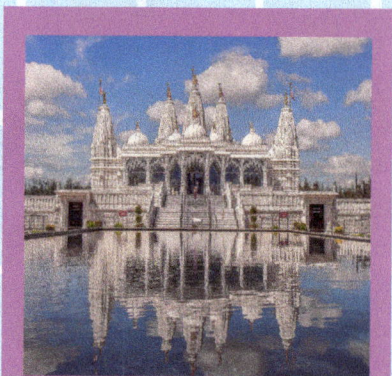

"Houston."

In 1969, it was the first word spoken from the moon!

33,000

That's how many pieces of marble were used to piece together Houston's Shri Swaminarayan Mandir, the largest Hindu temple in Texas.

Houston First

The Astrodome was the first covered stadium in the United States. It opened in 1965.

No.1

In space for urban parks among cities with more than 1 million people

145

Languages spoken by people who live in or near Houston

25%

That's about how many citizens of Houston were born outside the United States.

No.1

People in Houston eat out more often than folks in any other US city!

Not Far Away

Whether you live in Houston or you're just visiting the city, don't forget that many other awesome places to visit are very close by. Get a driver and hit the road for these fun day (or so!) trips.

We hit the road! Headed south to Galveston to get some beach time.

Cool! Is that on the Gulf?

Yup. Gulf of Mexico. This Pleasure Pier is packed with stuff to do—Ferris wheel, roller-coaster, cotton candy, the whole amusement park.

🤭 Jealous!

Plus there are miles of great beaches to walk on. It's a great way to escape the city for fresh air!

We also took a ride on this ship.

Where's the motor?

LOL! It's a sailing ship called the *Elissa*. It's 150 years old. We had to help put up the sails and everything!

Work . . . and play!

Next stop, Big Thicket National Preserve. It's in an area called Piney Woods.

It looks cool . . . and wet!

Those are called bayous. We took a boat trip to see the birds and other critters that live there.

Did you paddle?

We took an airboat, but there were also canoes and kayaks to rent.

The whole Piney Woods area is still a place where they do logging. But people are planting more trees to make sure birds like these have a place to live.

Tweet, tweet (the bird kind!)

Not Far Away

Hi! I'm writing to you from the city of Austin!

A capital idea!

Ha! Good one! That's right, it's the Texas state capital. It's about a three-hour drive from Houston.

Depending on traffic!

Right, but once you get there you can visit the State Capitol building and see where Texas makes its laws.

I vote yes!

Austin is also home to a very cool group of bats.

Baseball or vampire?

Ha! Neither. Just regular bats. In spring and summer, a huge group flies out at dusk from under a bridge in Austin.

That's a lot of bats!

It was awesome. And then we heard some great music downtown.

Another big ship! This one DOES have engines! It's the USS *Lexington*!

IT'S HUGE!

It's an aircraft carrier that was used in World War II. We toured the whole ship and saw the planes on the deck.

Aye-aye, skipper!

While we were in Corpus Christi, we also went to the Texas State Aquarium

Splish-splash! Say hi to the dolphins!

Sister Cities Around the World

Did you know cities can have sisters? Why not brothers? Well, that's just what they're called. Sister Cities was started in 1956 as a program of the U.S. government. The idea was to connect cities here and around the world to help people get to know each other. Today, Houston has 18 international "sisters"!

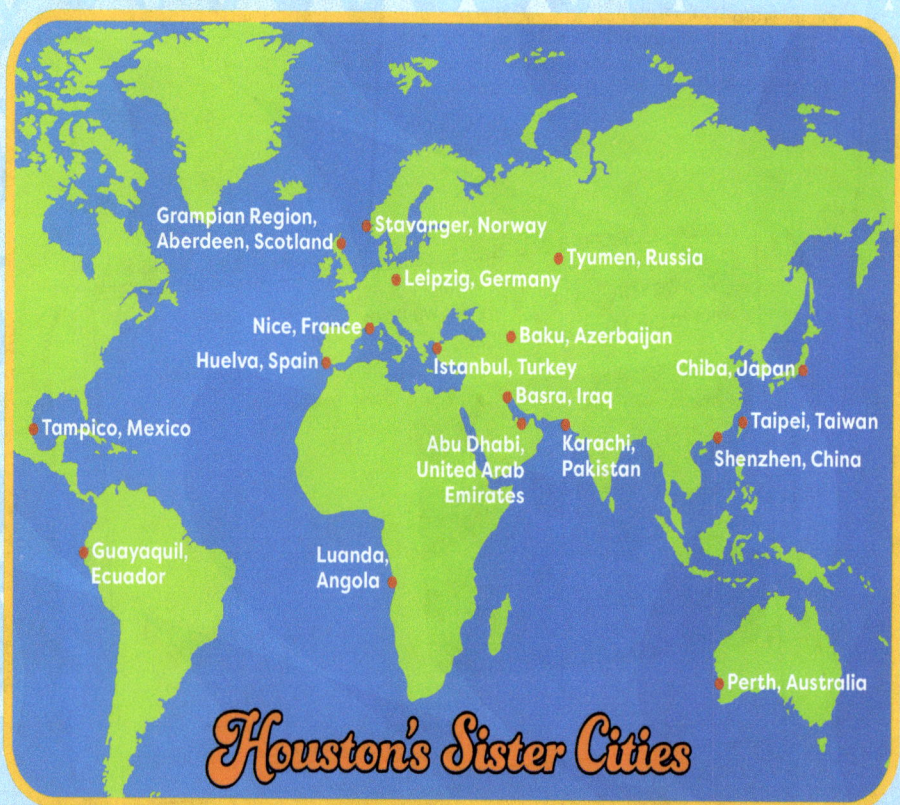

Grampian Region, Aberdeen, Scotland

Stavanger, Norway

Leipzig, Germany

Tyumen, Russia

Nice, France

Baku, Azerbaijan

Huelva, Spain

Istanbul, Turkey

Chiba, Japan

Basra, Iraq

Tampico, Mexico

Abu Dhabi, United Arab Emirates

Karachi, Pakistan

Taipei, Taiwan

Shenzhen, China

Guayaquil, Ecuador

Luanda, Angola

Perth, Australia

Houston's Sister Cities

Sister Cities in Action

Here are some examples of how Houston and its residents work with and help their Sister Cities:

Baku: Thanks to the Sister Cities program, college students from Baku can study at several Houston colleges, and young Houstonians have a chance to study in Baku.

Karachi: Through the program, residents of the two sister cities worked together to provide a water pump to needy people in Pakistan. The pump provides clean water to 60,000 people every day!

Taipei: Residents of this sister city gave Houston a special gift. In 1976, the United States celebrated its 200th birthday. To mark that special occasion, Taipei donated a building called a pavilion. You can find it in Houston's Memorial Park.

Abu Dhabi: Several of Houston's sisters are in countries with mostly Muslim residents, such as Abu Dhabi. They follow the Islamic religion. Those cities and Houston have teamed up to collect food for Houston Muslims. The food is eaten during a special Islamic meal called Iftar.

Books, Websites, and More!

Books

Davis, Brian M. *Lost Galveston.* Mount Pleasant, SC: Arcadia Publishing, 2010.

Mary Dodson. *Sam Houston: I Am Houston.* Houston: Bright Sky Press, 2009.

DuTerroil Dana, and Joni Fincham, *111 Places in Houston That You Must Not Miss.* Cologne, Germany: Emons Verlag, 2020.

Powell, William Dylan. *Secret Houston: A Guide to the Weird, Wonderful, and Obscure.* St. Louis: Reedy Press 2019.

Web Sites

Visit Houston
https://www.visithoustontexas.com/

City of Houston
http://www.houstontx.gov/

Lonely Planet: Houston
https://www.lonelyplanet.com/usa/texas/houston

NASA Space Center
https://spacecenter.org/

Houston Livestock Show and Rodeo
https://www.rodeohouston.com/

25 Fun Things to Do in Houston with Kids
https://familydestinationsguide.com/fun-things-to-do-houston-kids/

Photo Credits and Thanks

Photos from Dreamstime, Library of Congress, Shutterstock, or Wikimedia unless otherwise noted. Alamy: Zhang Yongxing/Xinhua/Alamy Live News 31. Texas Wildlife Rehabilitiation Center: 79

Artwork: LemonadePixel; danceyourlife. Maps (6-7): Jessica Nevins.

Cultural Content Consultant: Jennifer E. Ellwood.

Thanks to our pal Nancy Ellwood and the fine folks at Arcadia!

INDEX

Thanks for Visiting

HOUSTON

Come Back Soon!